MARY MAGDALENE'S STATIONS OF THE CROSS

ANN REGIMBAL

Copyright © 2020 by Ann Regimbal

All rights reserved. This book or any portion thereof may not be reproduced or used in any manner whatsoever without the express written permission of the author/publisher except for the use of brief quotations in a book review.

ISBN 978-1-7347190-1-7 Paperback

ISBN 978-1-7347190-2-4 Hardcover

ISBN 978-1-7347190-0-0 eBook

Ann Regimbal

New York, New York

www.annregimbal.com

To contact the author/publisher regarding bulk orders, speaking engagements (in person or via webinar) or for any other inquiries relating to this book, please email Ann at: ann@annregimbal.com.

To My Wonderful Mother and Father

"If you had to write a book about something, I'm glad you wrote a book about God."
-John Kenneth Behan (my father), age 96

My incredible friends,
who have been a great source of encouragement:
Daniela Liscio, Veronica Pastor, Blair and Jewel Walker, Patricia O'Connell, Kathleen Camilli, Angela Weissenberger, Lilla Runco, Deborah Rosati, Irene Winel, Sihin Gebregiworgis, Alison Jeffrey, Mike Konig, Sylvia Chrominska, Jill and Kim Nixon – and so many others!

And the terrific people I've met on the Magdala Project,
especially Father Eamon Kelly, L.C. and Jennifer Ristine.

Very special thanks to my wonderful client in Israel,
without whom I would never have had the opportunity to visit Tel Aviv, Jerusalem, Magdala, Caesarea Maritime and so many amazing places filled with history.
You are the BEST!

And sincere thanks to Chrissy Hobbs of Indie Publishing -
For her invaluable help and guidance on this book.

MARY MAGDALENE'S STATIONS OF THE CROSS

CONTENTS

Before we Begin ix
The Stations of the Cross
    Station One: Jesus is Condemned to Death. 1
    Station Two: Jesus Takes Up His Cross 5
    Station Three: Jesus Falls the First Time 8
    Station Four: Jesus Meets His Mother. 10
    Station Five: Simon of Cyrene Helps Jesus Carry the Cross   12
    Station Six: Veronica Wipes the Face of Jesus 14
    Station Seven: Jesus Falls a Second Time. 18
    Station Eight: Jesus Speaks to the Women of Jerusalem. 21
    Station Nine: Jesus Falls a Third Time. 25
    Station Ten: Jesus is Stripped of His Garments 27
    Station Eleven: Jesus is Nailed to the Cross. 29
    Station Twelve: Jesus Dies on the Cross. 31
    Station Thirteen: Jesus is Taken Down from the Cross. 35
    Station Fourteen: Jesus is Laid in the Tomb. 40
Easter Saturday and Easter Sunday
    Easter Saturday. 47
    Easter Sunday. 50
What Does Recent Archeology Tell Us About Mary Magdalene?
    Magdala Today: A Place that Honors Women 65
Bibliography. 70

BEFORE WE BEGIN

The Beauty of Mary Magdalene

I have tremendous admiration for Mary Magdalene—and if you're reading these pages, perhaps you do as well. She faced the tragedy of Christ's passion with courage, loyalty, and fortitude—qualities Mary Magdalene displays throughout the entire Easter story, right up until that morning, two days later, when she stands before the open tomb.

Mary Magdalene's character has long been associated with penitence. This tradition resulted from a homily delivered by Pope Gregory the Great in the 6th century that confused Mary Magdalene with the unnamed 'sinful woman' who washes Jesus' feet in repentance and Mary of Bethany, who does likewise. When you read the Bible, itself, however a very different image of Mary Magdalene emerges—a woman who is strong, brave, determined, and virtually unstoppable! She is someone with character traits that many women today aspire to, a saint for the 21st century.

Artists typically portray Mary Magdalene as a beautiful woman. This has largely stemmed from the age-old confusion that she was a 'sinful woman' and therefore an object of desire. But Mary Magdalene most certainly was beautiful—for she had a beautiful and courageous spirit. She fearlessly stood by the people she loved and believed in.

Every time I pray the Stations of the Cross, I think about Mary Magdalene: Where was *she* standing? What was *she* thinking as each of these dreadful events unfolded before her eyes? Because Mary Magdalene was there. And she stayed until the bitter end.

The Powder Keg of Jerusalem

The political backdrop against which the events of Christ's passion unfold is a fundamental component of the Stations. For this reason, some discussion of historical events, findings from recent archeology and even subsequent legends about the people who play a role in the Stations have been incorporated into this book. Let's begin with a short discussion of the tempestuous politics brewing in Judea at the time of Jesus.

The Roman Empire had conquered Judea and people living there resented their subjugation to a foreign power. They prayed for a Messiah to overthrow the Romans and set the country free, just as Moses had freed the people of Israel from the Egyptians.

The Romans used the Herod family as puppet kings. The Herods may have been the rulers of Judea, but they were obedient to Rome and constantly in fear of being overthrown.

Herod the Great ruled Judea at the time of Jesus' birth. He is alleged to have ordered the death of all male infants (the Massacre of the Innocents) so as to slay the prayed-for Messiah before he grew to adulthood. This resulted in the flight into Egypt by Jesus' family. While some scholars dispute that the Massacre of the Innocents actually took place, there is no doubt that Herod was ruthless in thwarting anyone who threatened his power; he even executed several members of his own family, including his wife.

Herod the Great is also the ruler who built the Second Temple in Jerusalem. This is the Temple that Jesus visited as a child and where he threw out the money-changers later in life. Today, the Western Wall (or Wailing Wall) in Jerusalem is all that remains of this once magnificent building.

When Herod the Great died, the country was divided between his two sons: Herod Philip and Herod Antipas. Herod Antipas established his court at Tiberius on the shore of the Sea of Galilee, close to the prosperous town of Magdala. It is Herod Antipas who appears in the stories of Jesus' ministry. Like his father, Herod Antipas was fearful of anyone who might pose a challenge to his authority, such as John the Baptist, whom he beheaded.

Interestingly, another of Jesus' female followers is a woman named Joanna. She is described as the wife of Herod's steward, Chuza (Luke 8:3). The role of steward would be tantamount to running Herod's household and financial affairs, suggesting that Joanna would have been a woman of high social status in the Galilee region. Joanna travelled to Jerusalem with Jesus and Mary Magdalene. The Gospel of Luke even states that she accompanied Mary Magdalene to Jesus' tomb on Easter morning and was one of the witnesses to the Resurrection (Luke 24:10). One can't help but wonder if Joanna stayed at Herod's palace in Jerusalem during this visit.

In addition to supporting the Herodian family in ruling over parts of Judea, the Roman Emperor also appointed a procurator, or governor, to the region to enforce Roman authority and protect Roman interests. Pontius Pilate was the fifth Governor of Judea appointed since the Roman occupation. Pilate held this post for roughly ten years, from about 26–36 CE.

Pilate was responsible for keeping order. This included putting down any uprisings against Roman authority. Plots of this nature were constantly fomenting, with much talk of a Messiah being sent by God to set the Jewish people free. Acts of rebellion in defiance of Rome were typically put down in cruel and vicious ways designed to instill fear in others who might have similar aspirations. Crucifixion was one of these methods.

Pilate did not live in Jerusalem. He lived in the magnificent city of Caesarea Maritime on the coast of the Mediterranean (near modern-day Haifa). Caesarea was an elegant and cosmopolitan city constructed in the Roman style by Herod the Great. It included a massive amphitheater, a stadium for chariot races, baths/spas, and an aqueduct, which can still be seen today. Caesarea was an important hub for international trade; out of its port, goods from Judea and surrounding areas were shipped across the Mediterranean Sea to Rome.

The feast of Passover is held every spring, and Jewish people from all over the country came to Jerusalem to worship at the Temple. The Roman authorities were particularly on edge at this time. After all,

Passover celebrates an event that secured the liberation of the people of Israel from the Egyptians. As such, the celebration of this event might stoke popular fervor towards Jewish liberation from Rome. With so many people gathered in the city, there was tremendous potential for trouble to break out. This is why Pontius Pilate came to Jerusalem during the Passover festival.

One final and critical dimension in the Judean power scheme of the time involved the Jewish religious leaders. The high priest of the Temple was a man named Joseph Caiaphas. Caiaphas and the Jewish religious establishment were undoubtedly rattled by Jesus' teachings and activities, including throwing the money-changers out of the Temple and preaching a radically different theology to his followers than the traditional Jewish views.

The Sanhedrin, a senior council of Jewish elders, was also part of the religious power structure of the time. This body had the authority to conduct trials and administer Jewish law. However, the Sanhedrin could not exercise capital punishment even if the Jewish law required it; only the Romans could put someone to death.

All three major powers at the time—Rome, Herod, and the Sanhedrin—had concerns about Jesus. But it was Caiaphas and the religious leaders who undoubtedly felt most threatened by him.

It is into this powder-keg that Jesus and his followers descend as they enter the city of Jerusalem on Palm Sunday of 33 CE. All of these factors played into the sequence of events that followed: Jesus' arrest at Gethsemane, his trial before the Sanhedrin, his appearance before Herod, and his second trial before the Roman governor, Pontius Pilate, where he was condemned to death.

The Via Dolorosa

In 326 CE, a seventy-six-year-old woman embarked on a journey to Jerusalem to discover the actual sites of Jesus' tomb and crucifixion. Her name was Helena, or St. Helen as she's more popularly known. The volcano in Washington State known as Mount St. Helens is named in her honor.

Helena was the mother of the Roman Emperor Constantine, who de-criminalized Christianity in 313 CE. Helena, herself, was a practicing Christian before the religion was legalized.

Helena was accompanied on her quest to the Holy Land by a legion of soldiers furnished by her son. There are many legends about Helena's trip to Jerusalem and her discovery of the true cross during her visit. But we will focus instead on her discovery of the sites that form part of the Stations of the Cross today.

Helena was informed that the site of Calvary was a former rock quarry and that Jesus' tomb, nearby, lay beneath a temple to the Roman goddess Venus built by the Emperor Hadrian about 135 CE. Helena's team of soldiers demolished the temple and discovered a rock-cut tomb beneath it, which Helena and Macarius, Bishop of Jerusalem at the time, identified as Jesus' place of burial.

Constantine ordered a church built over these two holy sites for protection and reverence. This became the Church of the Holy Sepulcher in Jerusalem. The church today incorporates both sites (Calvary, where Jesus died on the cross, and Jesus' tomb). It is one of the most popular and important pilgrimage sites in the Christian world.

Helena also brought back from her visit to Jerusalem a set of stairs known as the Scala Sancta, which pilgrims to Rome visit today. These were stairs that Helena believed Jesus ascended for his trial before Pontius Pilate at the praetorium in Jerusalem. Many scholars believe that the praetorium was located at the Antonio Fortress, which housed the Roman garrison in Jerusalem at the time.

This is the reason why the Via Dolorosa (the Way of Sorrows) in Jerusalem begins at the former location of the Antonio Fortress and proceeds through the narrow streets of the Old City to the Church of the Holy Sepulcher.

The Stations of the Cross that you see today in churches around the world are all representations of the Via Dolorosa in Jerusalem. They were originally built outdoors to allow Europeans who had no chance of visiting the original sites in the Holy Land to take part in this pilgrimage experience. Some had up to thirty sites (as opposed to the traditional fourteen Stations of the Cross today).

Stations of the Cross provide an opportunity for reflection and meditation on Christ's passion. They are typically undertaken during the Easter season, most commonly Good Friday. However, some people find it preferable to pray the Stations of the Cross on their own and at a time of their choosing. This way, they can immerse themselves in meditative thought without feeling rushed or distracted by a more formal process.

In 1521, a German book entitled *Geystlich Strass* (the spiritual way) came into print, which included illustrations of the holy sites, themselves. The book you are now reading has been designed to provide a similar experience to readers five hundred years later, using current photos from present-day Jerusalem.

The Stations of the Cross can sometimes feel a bit formulaic, even dogmatic. But they shouldn't. This was an event full of raw and painful emotion, capped by the completely unexpected joy of the Resurrection.

This version has been designed to give a human voice—and a female voice, that of Mary Magdalene—to the Stations of the Cross, in the hopes of creating a profound and beautiful experience that touches the heart and enriches the mind. After all, this is what the creators of the Stations of the Cross always wanted those who undertook it to achieve.

THE STATIONS OF THE CROSS

STATION ONE:
Jesus is Condemned to Death

The Church of the Condemnation, Via Dolorosa, Jerusalem –
Traditional Site of the First Station of the Cross

BY THE TIME I arrive at the praetorium, there is already a large crowd assembled outside. This is the place where Pontius Pilate conducts trials when he is in Jerusalem. They are as much for show as they are for justice.

But I do have some hope: perhaps the people in this crowd include many of those who welcomed us into Jerusalem last Sunday, singing praises and spreading palm leaves. Maybe they will speak out in His favor.

Soon, however, those hopes are dashed. I can hear people talking amongst themselves, accusing Jesus of blasphemy, a crime deserving death. I realize that this crowd was amassed by Caiaphas, the high priest, to ensure the result he wants. And he wants Jesus' death.

Pilate appears and beside him stands Jesus, though I can barely recognize Him. He is bloody and beaten, with shackles on His wrists. His garments are covered with streaks of blood that belie the use of a whip.

Pilate addresses the crowd. "In keeping with tradition, I will release to you a prisoner for Passover to show my leniency and generosity of spirit, and that of the Emperor. Which prisoner shall it be? This man, Jesus, who you call the King of the Jews? Or Barabbas, who led riots in the city and stands convicted of murder?"

For one short moment, my heart is alive with hope. "Jesus!" I cry out. "Give us Jesus!"

But my voice is quickly drowned out by the crowd who all yell "Barabbas! Barabbas! Give us Barabbas!"

"What, then, shall be done with this man, Jesus?" Pilate asks, "I find no fault in him."

"Crucify him!" the crowd shouts back. "Crucify him!"

In the crowd are some of the high priests. One of them shouts loudly, "We have a law. And according to that law, he ought to die because he claimed to be the son of God." (John 19:7-8)

"Do you want me to crucify your king?" Pilate responds. The chief priests answer, "We have no king except for Caesar." (John 19: 15-16)

"Crucify him! Crucify him!" the crowd keeps chanting. I pray that Pilate will send his soldiers out to quiet the mob—and set Jesus free. He has found no fault in Him and knows there is no basis to put Him to death.

Instead, Pilate gives way to the mob. He orders a servant to bring him a basin of water and washes his hands theatrically before the crowd. "I am innocent of this man's blood," he states. (Matthew 27: 25)

Then, he speaks the words of condemnation: Jesus must be put to death by crucifixion, the most horrible death imaginable. Does Pilate really think washing his hands of the matter absolves him of the death of an innocent man in a horrific way?

REFLECTIONS AND PRAYERS

- ❖ When I witness terrible injustice, as Mary Magdalene saw before her, I pray for the courage to raise my voice and try to make a difference — even if I am drowned out by the crowd.

- ❖ I ask God's forgiveness for those instances where I have failed to speak up for someone or for something that I believed in and I pray for the strength to do so when such opportunities arise again.

What and Where was the Praetorium?

The term 'praetorium' historically referred to a military general's tent. However, it could also refer to an administrative center.

Because of its military association, many scholars believe the praetorium would have been at the Antonia Fortress, where the Roman garrison in Jerusalem was stationed. However, if it referenced an administrative center, this may have been part of Herod's palace in Jerusalem, near the present site of the David Tower.

In 2015, an Israeli archaeologist discovered a 1ˢᵗ century prison cell near the David Tower, lending credence to the theory that *this* was the actual site of Jesus' trial by Pilate. If scholars increasingly subscribe to this view, the Stations of the Cross/Via Dolorosa may eventually change, so as to begin at the David Tower. However, this book follows the traditional Stations of the Cross on the Via Dolorosa in Jerusalem today.

Who was Pontius Pilate?

Little is known about Pontius Pilate's early life, although it is likely that he ascended through the ranks of the Roman military and was eventually named procurator (governor) of Judea by the Emperor Tiberius in 26 CE. He served in this role for ten years.

In his capacity as Roman governor, Pilate had the authority to appoint the High Priest of the Temple. Joseph Caiaphas was already serving in this role at the time that Pilate arrived in Judea and Pilate kept him in place throughout his tenure.

Not long after he came to Judea, Pilate angered the Jewish authorities by bringing busts of the emperor, attached to military standards, into Jerusalem. Jewish law forbids the making of images, something previous Roman governors understood and avoided. When the Jewish authorities asked Pilate to remove the busts he refused, whereupon Jewish demonstrators prostrated themselves outside Pilate's home in Caesarea for five days and nights.

On the sixth day, a ring of Roman soldiers surrounded the protestors and drew their swords, threatening them with death if they did not disperse. The protestors bared their necks, declaring they would rather die than transgress the Jewish law. Impressed with the religious zeal of the Jewish demonstrators, Pilate called off his soldiers and transferred the busts back to Caesarea.

This incident is often referenced by scholars to explain Pilate's decision to crucify Jesus rather than risk another uprising of the Jewish people, who claimed that their laws had been violated by Jesus.

STATION TWO:
Jesus Takes Up His Cross

Monastery of the Flagellation, Via Dolorosa, Jerusalem –
Traditional Site of the Second Station of the Cross

JESUS IS BROUGHT into the courtyard in a purple cloak. A hideous crown fashioned out of thorns has been placed upon His head. It digs into His flesh and blood streams down His face. The soldiers mock Him as the King of the Jews, kneeling down before Him. They spit on Him and slap Him.

I raise my eyes and pray with all my strength for some intervention from God to end all of this. I have seen so many miracles—people raised from the dead, people cured of terrible illness—and I beg for just one more.

The crowd mocks Him. "You saved others! Save yourself! Prove to us that you are the Messiah!" I do not need proof; I believe in Him.

Across the yard, soldiers drag in a wooden cross. This will be the instrument of His further torture—and His death. What is more, He will be forced to carry it to the place of execution outside the city walls. They bring the cross towards Him and remove His cloak. The crowd falls silent. They wait for Him to take up the cross.

He closes His eyes and I think that He must be praying—for strength, for help from God. I know that God hears Him, and I look to see the Hand of God reaching down to destroy the cross, to vanquish the mocking soldiers and to send all the others running in fear. But this does not occur.

His eyes reopen and He reaches out, taking the cross and bracing it on His shoulder. He realizes that He must go on. I believe in my heart that God will save Him. But for some reason there is still more suffering and humiliation for Him to endure.

At that moment, I make a vow. I vow not to abandon Him as Peter and the others have done. I lack the power to stop these atrocities. But I have the power to stay - and to comfort Him if I can, with my presence and my love- to the end of these ordeals.

And so, the walk to Calvary begins.

REFLECTIONS AND PRAYERS

- ❖ Mary Magdalene makes a vow to stay with Jesus to the end. She realizes that she cannot change the course of events, but draws on the power she has: The power to support and comfort.

- ❖ I thank God for all those who have stayed by my side throughout my own ordeals. And I ask for the strength to stay with and comfort others, when they need me.

STATION THREE:
Jesus Falls the First Time

UNSTEADY AND BAREFOOT, with the heavy cross against His bloodied shoulder, He steps forward. The Roman soldiers gather around, shepherding Him out into the street. One of them, a centurion, is on horseback, pushing the crowds aside as they clamor to watch.

He is weakened from being whipped and beaten; the cross is awkward and heavy. Every step must be an agony. The crowds in the street are jeering, "Hail King of the Jews! Let us all bow down before you!"

I follow behind. Amidst the crowds, I lose sight of Him as He turns a corner into the next street. Then I hear a commotion and race ahead, pushing my way between the onlookers.

He has fallen and lies in the road. His strength has given way under the terrible burden.

"Get up!" the soldiers order Him, their tones harsh.

In that moment, I have also fallen—not down onto the street, but in my heart. For my faith is shaken. I cannot understand why God would allow this to happen! When will this torment end? And will it end in a moment of glory, as I fervently pray and want to believe? Or only in derision and pain?

He struggles to His feet. He lifts the heavy cross back upon His shoulder. He continues on. And so do I.

REFLECTIONS AND PRAYERS

- ❖ I reflect upon the times where I have fallen—where I have lost faith.

- ❖ Dear God, forgive me for doubting you. Help me to know that you are always there. Give me strength, even in dark and trying times, to pick up my burden, no matter how heavy it may seem, and carry on.

STATION FOUR:
Jesus Meets His Mother

THERE SHE STANDS, in loveliness and grace: His mother, Mary. Her beautiful face is drawn with worry and creased with pain from seeing her beloved son in such distress—brutally tortured and condemned to a merciless death.

It must break her gentle heart to see Him in this way. Yet I feel sure that her loving presence must help to ease His pain amidst everything that He must now endure. For that I am grateful.

She steps away from the crowd and comes towards Him. She gazes into His eyes with so much tenderness in her sorrowful expression. He looks at her with love and pity, knowing the terrible heartache she must be feeling at this awful moment. Yet the bond between them is so strong and beautiful that even now, amidst the horror of this day, it transcends all that is happening.

She leans in to whisper something to Him. No one can hear the words that pass between them. I wonder what it is that she has said. What can a mother say to her son, who has been betrayed, beaten, and unjustly condemned to death, walking in anguish, bearing a cross to His execution?

Of this I am certain: Mary found the right words. Her heart must be torn in pieces, her eyes burning with tears. She might have condemned all of the injustice at hand. Instead, she radiated love.

REFLECTIONS AND PRAYERS

- ❖ Mary brings love—to a scene filled with anguish, brutality, and denigration. Although she is surely devastated by the fate of her beloved son, rather than bewail this cruelty or shake her fists in outrage, Mary chooses love.

- ❖ I reflect on people who have chosen love at the very moment when most others would have chosen anger and condemnation. I vow to look for opportunities to choose love rather than recriminations where difficulties emerge in my own life.

STATION FIVE:
Simon of Cyrene Helps Jesus Carry the Cross

HE NEARLY FALLS once more and braces against a wall to keep His balance. The centurian calls out to a man in the crowd who has just entered from the city gates up ahead. He is a dark-skinned man from abroad who appears to have his sons with him.

"Simon!" I hear the centurion call to him, "Come and help us here!"

The man stops and looks up at the centurion. He's clearly displeased with being interrupted on his way into the city and being instructed to take on an onerous task.

"This condemned man is unable to carry his cross to the place of execution. You must help him!"

The man named Simon seems bewildered and annoyed by this request. But a centurion's order is not to be disregarded. So he stops. He turns to Jesus and sees His terrible suffering.

In that moment, Simon's heart opens—to a stranger, to a prisoner condemned to death—to our Lord. Simon passes the baggage he was carrying over to one of his sons. He then reaches down and helps take up the cross. "Here," he says to Jesus, "I will help you."

REFLECTIONS AND PRAYERS

❖ When I see someone in despair, someone who needs my help, let my heart be open. Let me turn to him or her as Simon of Cyrene turned to Jesus on that terrible day and say, "Here, I will help you."

Who Was Simon of Cyrene?

Simon of Cyrene was a passerby enlisted by the Roman soldiers to help Jesus carry His cross. Cyrene was a town in North Africa, near modern-day Libya. For this reason, Simon of Cyrene is often portrayed as a dark-skinned man. However, his actual ethnicity is unknown.

STATION SIX:
Veronica Wipes the Face of Jesus

A DOORWAY OPENS AND a woman steps out into the street.

She is startled by the wretched sight before her: Jesus, bruised and bloody, struggling to walk; the centurion before Him on horseback; Roman soldiers surrounding Him; and Simon following behind, carrying the cross.

The woman pauses to take it all in. She meets His gaze and sees His anguish—and cannot bring herself to turn away. She wants to help Him but seems unsure of what to do.

Then she reaches up, takes the veil from her hair, folds it, and hands it to Jesus so that he may use it to wipe the blood and sweat from his face. She waits patiently as He does so, hoping that this moment will offer a brief respite from His pain.

It is a small mercy.

But, by this one gesture of kindness towards a suffering man, she has brought the balm of compassion to a moment of deep distress. Even the soldiers are moved and the crowd is hushed.

When He is done, she takes the veil back from His hand, offering Him a tender smile. Then she returns to the doorway from whence she came and goes back inside.

REFLECTIONS AND PRAYERS

❖ Veronica did not turn away from the suffering before her. She found a way to offer respite and mercy—and her gesture of compassion has been remembered throughout the centuries.

❖ Like Veronica, let me find ways to offer small acts of kindness throughout my day, never knowing what their impact might truly be. Even for a moment, let me bring compassion and warmth to those in difficulty who cross my path.

The Mystery of Veronica's Veil

The compassionate woman who wiped the face of Jesus on his way to Calvary was probably not named Veronica, even though she has been referred to by that name throughout history. The name is undoubtedly derived from the legend that an imprint of Jesus' face was left on her veil after this encounter. 'Vera' is the Latin word for true and 'Icon' is the Greek word for image, suggesting that she is the person who received the 'true image' of Christ.

There are currently six different artifacts in churches and palaces around the world that contend to be either the true veil of Veronica or a copy thereof. Scholars tend to refer to these items as 'the Veronica' suggesting that the term should be applied to the cloth itself, instead of the person who owned it.

One of the most interesting of these many 'Veronicas' is a veil rediscovered in 1999 at a Capuchin monastery in the Italian town of Manoppello by Professor Heinrich Pfeiffer, a Professor of Christian art at the Vatican's Gregorian University. Pfeiffer contends that the veil was stolen from the Vatican in 1608. At the time, there had been a renovation to St. Peter's Basilica involving the demolition of a chapel in which the veil had been stored.

A Trappist nun by the name of Blandina Paschalis Schlomer undertook an experiment to overlay the image on the Manoppello veil of Veronica against the image of the face found on the Shroud of Turin. She determined that the images on both cloths were of the same person. In the case of the Shroud of Turin, the man is dead, with his eyes closed. On the Manoppello veil, the same man appears alive, with his eyes open.

The Manoppello veil is made of a shimmering and transparent silken fabric. This fabric is byssus, or sea silk, a rare and extremely costly textile produced by weaving threads from the beards of a species of Mediterranean clam (the pinna nobilis).

Byssus was the most costly fabric of the ancient world. It has been found in the tombs of Egyptian pharaohs and is mentioned in the Bible as being used in the vestments of Jewish high priests. One interesting feature about byssus is that the fabric can be dyed but it is too fine to be painted upon. However, it is also considered too delicate for carbon-14 or other scientific testing to try to date it. Therefore, no such tests have ever been conducted.

Whoever Veronica was, if her veil really *is* the one in Manoppello, she was an extremely wealthy woman.

The Handprint of Jesus?

Embedded into the wall near Station Five, where Simon of Cyrene was called upon to assist Jesus, is a handprint that legend attributes to Jesus himself. The story goes that Jesus almost fell at this very spot and reached out to balance himself.

This prompted the Roman soldiers to find someone to help Jesus carry the cross, namely Simon of Cyrene.

A print was apparently created on the wall by Jesus' hand and it endures to the present day. It is one of the highlights for visitors to the Via Dolorosa in Jerusalem.

STATION SEVEN:
Jesus Falls a Second Time

WE CONTINUE ALONG the roadway, uphill towards the city gates. More women have joined the crowd, following along behind, weeping and lamenting. These women, I believe, may have been among those who welcomed Him into Jerusalem last Sunday.

How very long ago that day seems now! That was a day of triumph—a day of pure joy! Now, only five days later, the same man they greeted with cheers has become a condemned prisoner, walking painfully to His execution. Today, the crowds jeer and mock Him. They spit and laugh at Him. How quickly everything can change in this world—in only five days.

He has slowed His pace and I am able to move forward from the rear of the crowd. I am almost behind Simon now, as we reach the city gates. But there, He falls again.

"Get up!" I hear the Roman soldiers order Him.

He tries to lift Himself from the roadway, but His arms fail him and He falls back. The centurion reaches for the handle of his whip.

I race forward and kneel by the roadside, close to where He lies. I look up at the centurion and meet his eyes. Though I do not speak, he knows from my expression that I am begging him to show mercy. His face softens. He nods at me in quiet understanding and turns away.

By then, Jesus has recovered. He rises to His feet and walks forward.

The Lion Gate, Jerusalem

REFLECTIONS AND PRAYERS

❖ Mary Magdalene reflects upon the dramatic changes that have occurred since Palm Sunday—just five days earlier. So many things can cause our lives to take an unexpected and troubling turn: a diagnosis, the sudden death of a loved one, a divorce or break-up, the loss of a job.

❖ Dear St. Mary Magdalene, pray for me that I may have the strength to endure the sudden difficulties that will inevitably appear in my own life with the fortitude and courage with which you met the challenges that confronted you this terrible day.

STATION EIGHT:
Jesus Speaks to the Women of Jerusalem

A GROUP OF WOMEN, who have been following behind, now hurry forward to speak with Jesus. They realize that we are now approaching the Mount of Calvary, where He will be put to death.

These are women of Jerusalem, weeping and lamenting His fate.

But He tells them, "Daughters of Jerusalem, do not weep for me; weep rather for yourselves and for your children." (Luke 22: 28)

He predicts that the day will come when people will be happy never to have borne children because of the terrible ordeals that lie ahead. "Then they will begin to say to the mountains 'Fall on us!'; to the hills, 'Cover us!.'"(Luke 22:30–31)

The soldiers intervene and the women disperse. "This is no time for speeches," one of the Romans barks. "Get moving!" And He carries on as the roadway turns towards Calvary.

One of the women who had been in this group is sobbing by the city gates. I stop for a moment to talk with her. "Why are you crying?" I ask.

She replies, "I heard He was a miracle worker. And I prayed He was the Messiah! But now I have lost all hope. He is no Messiah, just a man; a man who now predicts more troubles to befall us."

REFLECTIONS AND PRAYERS

❖ Many people believed that a Messiah who could deliver their country from the Roman occupation would be the answer to all their troubles. But Jesus came to offer something far more profound than political freedom.

❖ Dear Lord, if I find myself disappointed in having been denied something I've prayed for, help me to see that a different and far more important solution to my problems may be at hand. Open my mind and my heart—and guide me with your grace.

The Great Revolt (66–70 CE)

Throughout the time of Jesus, the people of Jerusalem and other parts of Judea prayed for a Messiah to free their country from Roman occupation.

Three decades after Jesus' death (66 CE) a significant rebellion against Roman rule broke out in Judea, starting with riots in the coastal city of Caesarea Maritime. The Roman governor at that time, Gessius Florus, responded by plundering the Temple in Jerusalem for goods and money that he needed to fight the rebels. But this further infuriated the Jewish people and led to a wide-scale revolt throughout the country.

The Jewish rebels initially enjoyed great success. They even formed a provisional government in Judea which ruled the country during the years 66–68 CE. However, in 67 CE, Vespasian (who later became Roman Emperor) and his son, Titus, invaded the Galilee region and subdued the rebels in that area, including the town of Taricheae (the Greek name for Magdala, once home to Mary Magdalene). Historian Flavius Josephus described the conflict by saying that the Sea of Galilee "was red with blood, the shores strewn with swollen carcasses."

In 69 CE, Vespasian was recalled to Rome and named Emperor. His son Titus remained in Judea with his Roman military forces, which moved against Jerusalem one year later, in 70 CE. A lengthy siege ensued in which one of the Zealots (an extreme group of Jewish rebels) actually burned a supply of food in the city, believing that this would force the people of Jerusalem to fight harder against the Romans. Instead, it merely led to starvation.

By 71 CE, Jerusalem had fallen. The Temple was destroyed and three of its walls were demolished. Only one wall remained standing, which it does to this day: the Western Wall or Wailing Wall as it has come to be called. Jerusalem was burned and any survivors were taken into slavery by the Romans.

The remaining Jewish rebels took refuge at Masada, Herod's massive fortress near the Dead Sea. This became the final and legendary stronghold of the Jewish rebellion.

In 72 CE, the Romans mounted a siege at Masada. One year later, they breached the fortress, only to find that the defenders had chosen to commit mass suicide: 960 of the 967 people within were dead.

After the fall and burning of Jerusalem in 70 CE, the Romans rebuilt the city and named it Aelia Capitolina. They built a temple to the Roman god Jupiter on the Temple Mount, which infuriated Jews who still remained in the region.

Sixty years later (132–136 CE), another major Jewish revolt against Rome arose, led by Simon bar Kokhba. These rebels also enjoyed early successes and for two more years an independent Jewish state was created. Bar Kokhba was lauded as the Messiah, the man sent to restore Jewish independence.

However, the Roman Emperor Hadrian sent six Roman legions to Judea in 134 CE to put down the rebellion. It was crushed in 136 CE. The conflict and its aftermath devastated the Jewish people who, starting in 138 CE, were forbidden from entering the city of Jerusalem except for one day each year (Tisha B'Av, a sorrowful day of fasting).

Words of Jesus to the Women of Jerusalem

Most biblical scholars believe that the words of Jesus to the women of Jerusalem on the way his crucifixion prophesized these terrible events: the destruction of Jerusalem in 71 CE, the death and enslavement of her people, and the Jewish expulsion in 138 CE.

STATION NINE:
Jesus Falls a Third Time

The traditional site of the Ninth Station is marked with a circular brass plaque on the right. The blue dome in the distance (topped with a cross) is the Church of the Holy Sepulcher. It was built over the site St. Helena identified as Calvary during her trip to Jerusalem in the 4th century.

I HAVE FALLEN BEHIND and hurry to catch up. As I draw closer, He falls once again.

I realize then that I, too, have fallen—not here on the stony path leading to Calvary—but in my faith. For I have begun to doubt that God will save Him. And if not, then I pray that He will at least be spared the agonizing death of crucifixion! Let Him die here in the roadway. Free Him, at last, from even more torture and pain!

Finally, I near the front of the crowd, pushing even past Simon, who carries the cross. I can see Him struggling to rise once again, but His arms are so weary that it seems He cannot.

He looks up, surveying the faces of everyone in the crowd around Him. And He sees mine! There is a glint of recognition, a very soft smile slightly lifts the corners of His bloodied lips.

He gazes into my eyes, and I try to convey the words that I cannot bring myself to speak, "I believe in you, my teacher! I pray that this torture will end. I am here for you! I will never leave you!" His loving expression lets me know that He understands.

Then He turns away, pushes Himself upwards and stands once again. He breathes a deep sigh and takes a step forward.

The Roman soldiers surround him, goading him onwards to Calvary, which is now in view. Just then, He turns and looks back. He looks at me. And I, too, step forward and continue on.

REFLECTIONS AND PRAYERS

- ❖ Encouragement does not always require words. Sometimes only a look—filled with love, compassion and genuine support—can give us strength when we feel we simply cannot go on.

- ❖ I pray that I may be able to find ways to encourage those I care about, particularly at times when they are weary and losing hope. And I thank God for all those who have encouraged me.

STATION TEN:
Jesus is Stripped of His Garments

Station Ten and All Remaining Stations of the Via Dolorosa
are Located within the Church of the Holy Sepulcher.

FINALLY, WE ARRIVE at the place of the skull, known as Calvary. In the distance, I can see His mother, Mary, and some other women from the Galilee who came up to Jerusalem with us.

What wonders we all thought we'd see during this Passover visit—miracles and glories! Instead, we are here to witness the horrible death of the man who saved so many of us from terrible afflictions.

I go to the women and we embrace, weeping. I am so grateful to have them here; the horrors of this day are more than I can bear alone.

Then I turn and see that Jesus has been stripped of His garments. This is yet another humiliation He must bear: to stand before the crowd, naked. They do the same to two criminals standing nearby, preparing them for execution.

Four soldiers divide His clothing between them, hideous souvenirs. His undergarment is sewn from a single piece of cloth; for that, they cast dice.

My mind reflects back to a day where a woman once reached out to touch the hem of His garment as He walked in the marketplace. From that touch, she was cured of a hemorrhage that had afflicted her for years! But today, His garments are given little reverence.

REFLECTIONS AND PRAYERS

- ❖ Jesus' clothing—so holy that its very touch once cured a woman of a debilitating illness—is now divided between the Roman soldiers as a grim trophy. Something sacred is made profane.

- ❖ There can be times where things we hold dear—our beliefs, our values, our work, the people and things we care about—are trampled upon by others. When this happens, I pray for the courage to be steadfast and to keep those things I believe in close to my heart.

STATION ELEVEN:
Jesus is Nailed to the Cross

Mosaic depicting Jesus being nailed to the cross at the traditional site
of Station Eleven within the Church of the Holy Sepulcher

SOME OF THE soldiers pass Him a cup. It may be a mixture of myrrh offered to dull the terrible pain that awaits; a cup given in mercy. But He refuses to drink from it. He will suffer everything.

His cross is thrown on the ground and He is placed upon it, arms outstretched. One of the Roman soldiers picks up a heavy mallet and drives massive nails through His wrists. Blood spurts out. The pain must be excruciating! His feet are then nailed to the center beam, bones shattered, blood dripping down.

I cannot bear to watch. I close my eyes again and pray to God for mercy! Why hasn't God intervened to save Him? *Why?*

Then I hear Jesus' voice, sharp and clear, over the crowd. "Father, forgive them. They know not what they do!" (Luke 23:34)

He begs God's forgiveness for those who are torturing Him!

When I hear this, I realize that I must forgive as well. And if He must endure all this wretched suffering, then I can endure the watching of it. I will not look away again.

Then, His cross is raised. He is flanked on either side by the two criminals, robbers both. Above His head, they have nailed a sign: "Jesus of Nazareth—King of the Jews".

REFLECTIONS AND PRAYERS

- ❖ These simple words of Jesus, "Father, forgive them. They know not what they do", spoken at the very moment those for whom he begs forgiveness are putting him through excruciating pain is perhaps the most dramatic example of forgiveness in human history.

- ❖ Whenever I must withstand suffering, injustice, or any other difficulties that have been put upon me by someone that I feel I cannot forgive, I pray to remember these words—and the moment at which they were spoken.

STATION TWELVE:
Jesus Dies on the Cross

The altar marks the traditional site of the cross. The rocky white outcrop of Calvary can be seen on either side. There is a crack on the right side consistent with the biblical reference to "rocks splitting" at the moment of Jesus' death

H E HANGS UPON the cross in torment, awaiting death—a slow, wretched, horrid death. I have prayed all day that God would spare Him this anguish, that God would rescue Him—just as He rescued so many others from their suffering. But God has not heard my prayers.

There is a large crowd watching this horrible spectacle. Among them are some of the chief priests, here to witness the outcome of their heinous scheming, to see it through to its terrible end. Do they take pleasure in watching His suffering? Sadly, I believe that they do. How can they call themselves men of God?

My mind casts back to all those days of walking with Him on the shores of the Sea of Galilee, hearing Him teach. He seemed to know God, to understand God and what God wants of us. His was a God of love, a God that asked us to be grateful for our daily bread and treat each other the way that we would wish to be treated. And God gave Him the power to heal. How can this message of love and healing end with an agonizing death? He preached mercy, yet mercy has been denied to Him.

The crowd begins taunting Him, "So, you would destroy the Temple and rebuild it in three days?! Then save yourself! Come down from the cross!" they jeer. "He saved others. He cannot save himself. Let Christ, the King of the Jews, come down from the cross. Let us see it and believe!" (Mark 15: 29–32)

Even the robbers hanging beside him join in. "Are you not the Christ?" one asks, "Save yourself and us as well!" (Luke 23: 39–40)

But the other thief reprimands his friend, "Have you no fear of God? You got the same sentence as he did, but in our case, we deserved it. We are paying for what we've done. But this man has done nothing wrong." The thief then turns to the man beside him. "Jesus," he says to Him, "remember me when you come into your kingdom."

Jesus answers, "Indeed, I promise you—today you will be with me in paradise." (Luke 23: 40–43)

The other women around me are weeping and lamenting. His poor mother is nearly prostrate with grief! John, the young disciple Jesus loves, is with her. Barely a man, he is only about fifteen; Jesus has always treated him like a son. He loves all of us, of that I am convinced, but He loves John especially.

John is here; he has not fled like the others. Perhaps his youth has emboldened him. Or perhaps, like me, His love for Jesus is so great that nothing could persuade John to leave Him.

Jesus must see John comforting His mother, for He turns to both of them. "Woman, this is your son," He tells Mary, nodding towards John. And to John, "This is your mother." (John 19:26–27) He knows that John will heed His words and care for Mary in her old age with the love of a son for his mother.

Then He turns to me. He does not speak, nor do I wish it. Every word is an agony on the cross, for he must dig his pinioned feet into the crossbeam at great pain to fill his lungs. And there are no words to speak at this moment. He saved me from tremendous torment earlier in my life and while I cannot save him from the torment that He is now forced to suffer, I will not abandon him.

I struggle to avoid weeping. I want Him to see that my eyes remain full of hope, trusting always in Him. But this is difficult, for my hope is fading. Still, I relish this moment, gazing into those loving eyes filled with wisdom and mercy—perhaps for the last time. While I still want to believe that some miracle will yet occur, at this moment, I know that we are saying farewell.

The crowd has thinned out. Even some of the other women from the Galilee have left. I do not reproach them; watching Him die in agony is more than many can bear. Others in the crowd had also hoped to witness a breathtaking miracle. Instead, they have only watched a dying man endure terrible pain.

Finally, Jesus cries out in a loud voice, "My God, my God, why have you forsaken me?" (Matthew 27:47; Mark 15:24)

He, too, has now lost hope. When I hear His despair, I can hold back my own tears no longer. Yet, I wonder if His plaintive cry to God will yield the miracle that rescues Him, at last. For God listens to Him, of that I am certain. Why would God desert Him now?

Others in the crowd have the same thought. "He is calling on Elijah," they say, "Let us see if Elijah will deliver Him." Someone runs for a sponge filled with vinegar and holds it up to Him on a reed to drink. (Matthew 27:47–50)

But nothing happens. The heavens do not open; the earth does not tremble; the thunderous voice of God does not rebuke the chief priests and the Roman soldiers, nor send them all to a hideous fate in retribution for what they have done. God has ignored His heartfelt plea and left Him to die.

Finally, Jesus cries out, "Father, into your hands I commit my spirit!" (Luke: 23:46). He bows His head and breathes His last.

A great darkness descends. The earth quakes and rocks are split. For a moment, I wonder if this is the end of the world.

The centurion, who had accompanied Jesus on horseback and remained throughout His crucifixion, now falls to one knee, exclaiming, "Truly, this man *was* the son of God!" (Mark 15:39)

Then all is still once more.

REFLECTIONS AND PRAYERS

❖ Dear Lord, I can never begin to express all of my heartfelt gratitude for the suffering you endured upon the cross for my salvation—and that of all mankind.

STATION THIRTEEN:
Jesus is Taken Down from the Cross

The orange-colored stone, above, is the Stone of Anointing. It was placed in 1810 over the site where it is believed Jesus's body was laid when removed from the cross and prepared for burial.

MANY PEOPLE LEAVE Calvary after these things occur. But I remain, along with a few other women. We want to see that He is given a proper burial, that His body is not left on the cross to decompose nor thrown into a pit, which is the Roman practice for executed criminals. This is the last mercy we can offer Him.

Salome tells me that a rich man from Arimathea named Joseph has gone to Pilate to ask for Jesus' body. I know Joseph, a virtuous man, and pray that he will be successful in his quest.

More Roman soldiers now arrive along with one of the chief priests. I can hear the priest giving instructions that the bodies need to be removed before sundown as this is the Preparation Day before the Sabbath. The two robbers are still alive, though barely. So, the soldiers break their legs to force their deaths. It is hideous to watch.

Then they come to Jesus. He is already dead. One of the soldiers pierces His side with a lance; blood and water flow out.

At that moment, Joseph of Arimathea appears. He is winded from walking fast and uphill. He begs a word with the centurion. It appears that Pilate has, indeed, given permission for Joseph to have the body of Jesus. After they speak, the centurion motions for a ladder and the soldiers assist Joseph in detaching Jesus' lifeless body from the nails and taking it down from the cross.

Another man, Nicodemus, now arrives. He is also a member of the Sanhedrin and someone who I believe was a secret follower of Jesus. He has some servants with him, bearing linen cloths and a huge weight of myrrh and aloes.

The servants put down their burdens and Nicodemus hurries to help Joseph carry Jesus' body. They lay Him down on a stone slab and begin to prepare Him for burial.

His mother, Mary, rushes over to where He lies. She kneels down and cradles His lifeless body in her loving arms. There are no words of comfort anyone can offer her; we are all silenced by this sorrowful moment of a grieving mother's tender love.

Finally, Joseph speaks to her softly, "We need to bury him before the sun goes down. There isn't much time." She nods, kisses her son's wounded hand and allows Joseph to take Him from her. John helps her up and, with a loving embrace, leads her away.

Joseph unwraps a long linen shroud and they place His body upon it. Nicodemus hurriedly sets about anointing Him with oils he has brought. While he does so, I venture into the nearby garden to gather up some flowers. Some of the other women join me in this. When we return, we place the flowers all around Him.

It is then that I see the bloodstains around His head, where the hideous crown of thorns had pierced Him. I see the whip marks all across His arms and shoulders that speak of brutal beatings before He was forced to carry His cross. There are holes in His wrists and feet where the large, sharp nails that held Him to the cross have made their terrible marks. And there's the bloody wound in His side, where He was pierced with the lance. I stare in disbelief, struggling to comprehend all of the agony He endured.

Joseph folds the shroud over Him. "The sun is setting," he tells us. "We must lay him in the tomb before it does."

REFLECTIONS AND PRAYERS

❖ How do we say good-bye to someone we love? To someone who has made a difference in our lives?

❖ We often reflect on what they were forced to endure, whether ravaged by disease, the victim of an accident, perhaps even a tragic instance where they took their own life or had it taken from them.

❖ Dear St. Mary Magdalene, pray with me now for all those that I have loved and lost.

Who Was Joseph of Arimathea?

All four gospel writers describe Joseph of Arimathea as a rich man who went to Pilate to obtain Jesus' body after the crucifixion. Luke indicates that Joseph was a "member of the council"—likely a reference to the Sanhedrin—and that he "had not consented to what the others had planned and carried out." (Luke 23: 51) Beyond that, little is known about him.

Some scholars have speculated that Joseph may have been the Virgin Mary's brother or uncle. This belief stems from the Jewish custom requiring the nearest male relative to assist in the burial of a deceased person. Mary's husband, Joseph, appears to no longer be living by the time of Jesus' ministry, leading some scholars to hypothesize that Joseph of Arimathea was Jesus' closest male relative at the time.

It was customary for the Romans to throw the bodies of executed criminals into a common grave. To obtain Pilate's permission to give Jesus a private burial, some believe that Joseph must have demonstrated a claim consistent with the Jewish law.

Others, however, dispute this notion. They take the view that Pilate was already remorseful about sentencing Jesus to death and a request from a prominent member of the community to give Jesus a proper burial would probably not have met with much resistance.

Numerous legends have grown up around Joseph of Arimathea over the centuries. Some claim that he was a wealthy merchant who travelled frequently to the tin mines of Cornwall and that he brought Jesus with him to England when he was a teen. This was the inspiration for William Blake's 1804 poem, adapted to music in 1916 by Sir Hubert Perry to become the popular British hymn "Jerusalem":

> *And did those feet in ancient times*
> *Walk upon England's mountains green*
> *And was the holy Lamb of God*
> *On England's pleasant pastures seen*

Medieval legends claim that Joseph of Arimathea arrived in Glastonbury, England after the crucifixion, bringing with him the Holy Grail, the cup from the Last Supper, into which he had collected drops of Christ's blood while he was on the cross. These stories, which emerged in the 12th and 13th centuries, appear to have little validity. However, they became the cornerstone of Arthurian romances involving the quest for the Holy Grail.

Why are there Two Sites for Jesus' Tomb in Jerusalem Today?

The traditional site on the Via Dolorosa was identified by St. Helena during her visit to Jerusalem in the 4th century. This is the tomb pictured in Station Fourteen and the one most widely believed to be accurate. It is found inside the Church of the Holy Sepulcher, the same structure in which Calvary and the Anointing Stone (Stations Twelve and Thirteen) are located. Within the Church, the tomb is enclosed in a small house-like structure called the Edicule.

In 1883, British General Charles Gordon identified a second potential site near a hill in East Jerusalem which, in certain lighting, resembles a skull. This led him to believe that the hill was Calvary or Golgotha—the place of the skull. Several rock-hewn tombs were discovered in the area. The Garden Tomb, as this site is now called, is popular with Christian pilgrims to Jerusalem because the atmosphere evokes the imagery of Jesus' burial and resurrection. However, 20th century archaeologists have dated the Garden Tomb to the 8th-7th centuries BCE, which would render it too old to have served as the site of Jesus' burial.

STATION FOURTEEN:
Jesus is Laid in the Tomb

The site of Jesus' tomb inside the Church of the Holy Sepulcher

JOSEPH HAS ACQUIRED a rock-hewn tomb in a garden very near to Calvary. It is a new tomb that no one has yet been laid in. The garden around it is lovely. Somehow, I take comfort in this.

Joseph and Nicodemus manage to carry His body, wrapped in its shroud, to the sepulcher. It is not far. I follow along behind, as do the other Galilean women who still remain.

None of the women go into the tomb. I sit in the garden, looking up at the darkening sky. Often at such moments of reverie, I would pray to God. But at this moment, I have nothing to say. I wonder if I can ever pray again.

"Did you hear about the Temple?" Salome asks me. "When He died, the veil of the Temple was torn in two, split from top to bottom! Nicodemus was there. He told me about it."

There were many amazing things that happened when He died— the darkness, the earthquake, now the torn Temple veil. But that doesn't change the fact that He is gone and that He endured an agonizing death. I can think of nothing else.

Just then, Joseph and Nicodemus emerge from the tomb. Beside it is a large and heavy boulder. With some effort, they manage to roll it across the entranceway.

By now, it is evening and difficult to see. I have never previously set foot in this lovely garden. But I take note of exactly where His tomb is located—so that I might be able to find it again.

REFLECTIONS AND PRAYERS

❖ Let us conclude the Stations of the Cross with the traditional prayer of those who walk the Stations - whether on the Via Dolorosa in Jerusalem, in churches around the world, or in spirit.

❖ "We adore you, O Christ, and we Praise You Because by Your Holy Cross, You have Redeemed the World."

What Does the Shroud of Turin Tell Us about Jesus' Burial and Mary Magdalene's Role in It?

The Shroud of Turin

The Shroud of Turin is probably the most important Christian artifact in the world. It is a linen cloth roughly 14 feet in length imprinted with the image of a man who died by crucifixion. Experiments to prove its veracity as the burial cloth of Jesus are so numerous that the term 'sindonology' has been coined to refer to the science of Shroud study.

Carbon-14 Dating in 1988

Carbon-14 dating of the Shroud in 1988 determined that the linen fabric was produced in between the 13th and 14th centuries, suggesting a medieval forgery.

However, the results of the 1988 test have been criticized ever since. Carbon-14 dating has been proven inaccurate—by a thousand years in the case of an Egyptian linen cloth. Moreover, the Shroud was damaged in a fire in the 1530s. The fabric was singed and holes were created by drops of molten silver.

An order of French nuns repaired the Shroud two years later by sewing it onto a backing cloth and stitching twenty-two patches over the holes. Apparently, the Shroud sample used in the 1988 test was taken from one of the rewoven sections.

Two entirely different studies have found some interesting evidence that not only lend credence to the Shroud's authenticity, but may also provide some insights about the role of Mary Magdalene and others involved in Jesus' burial.

Coins Placed over the Eyes

In 1978, scientists using an image analyzer developed by NASA discovered "raised, button-like shapes over each eye" which appear to be coins. The letters and pictures on them were also visible through the lens of the NASA machine, allowing for identification of the types of coins used. The coin over the right eye was identified as a *dilepton lituus*, a coin minted between 29 and 32 CE at the direction of Pontius Pilate. It was a low-value coin of the smallest denomination, similar to a penny. The coin over the left eye was identified as a *lepton simpulum*, another coin minted by Pontius Pilate in 29 CE.

Assuming, of course, that the Shroud is genuine, this discovery suggests that one of the final acts performed by Joseph of Arimathea, Nicodemus, Mary Magdalene or someone else involved in Jesus's burial was that of placing of these coins on his closed eyes.

Flowers and Plants Placed Inside the Shroud

A fascinating study described by renowned Israeli botany professor Avinoam Danin in his book, *Botany of the Shroud*: *The Story of Floral Images on the Shroud of Turin* (2010) involved the analysis of hundreds of images of flowers, buds, fruits, stems, and leaves identified on the Shroud from a high-grade photograph made in 1931. This study was supplemented with an analysis of pollen grains taken from the Shroud in the 1970s.

The plants identified from this analysis were all found in the region of Israel. Moreover, Danin noted that four of the plant species could only be found together "in one place in the world", the area between Jerusalem and Hebron. In addition, nine of the species identified only flower in the months of March and April, consistent with the timing of Jesus' burial.

Assuming this is accurate, who would be the most likely person present at the burial to have gathered up these fresh flowers and plants, probably from the garden where the tomb was located? Who placed them on and around Jesus' body before He was wrapped in the linen cloth? Joseph of Arimathea, Nicodemus, or Mary Magdalene, and perhaps some of the other women?

Although anointing with flowers is not a traditional Jewish burial custom, scholars have suggested that flowers may have been used if scented oils were not available as a means of offsetting the inevitable odor that results as a body decays. This, in fact, may have been the reason that Mary Magdalene believed it was important to return to the tomb with myrrh on the Sunday morning and anoint the body properly.

John 19:38-40 tells us that Nicodemus "brought a mixture of myrrh and aloes weighing almost a hundred pounds" to Jesus' tomb. However, the group may have been too rushed or for some other reason may not have completed this part of the burial preparation in the appropriate way. Or, it may simply have been a case that Mary Magdalene wanted to replace the flowers or add more scented oils and spices to those already used in Jesus' burial.

The Church of the Holy Sepucher, Jerusalem

EASTER SATURDAY AND EASTER SUNDAY

Easter Saturday

The Garden of Gethsemane, Mount of Olives, Jerusalem

THIS DAY I spend alone and contemplate all that has occurred. I am weary and overwhelmed. My eyes are red and hollow; my tears are all poured out. My strength has left me.

I have no desire to go to the Temple or celebrate the Passover. Watching Caiaphas parade his piety and sacrifice his lambs to God is more than I can bear. He sent a lamb to slaughter on the cross. If the veil of the Temple has been torn in two, I am glad for it.

My very faith in God has been shaken. I ask myself time and again how God could let this happen, and to someone God so clearly loved and blessed. Then I wonder whether my faith was misplaced all along. Perhaps I wanted so much to believe that I convinced myself it was all true, that Jesus was the son of God, the beloved son who had come to teach us the right ways in which to truly please God.

Jesus threw off the yoke of arcane rules and spoke of true righteousness. He shone a bright light into the darkness of corruption - and there has been so much of it amongst the high priests, the very people who claim to serve God but serve only themselves. He was the light of the world! Well, He was the light in my world, at least, and in the world of many others. Oh, how I wanted to believe in Him!

Surely He was touched by God, if not God incarnate! For how else was He able to drive away my own torments, to heal others who were sick, to cure the lame, to bring the dead back to life? Yet, He could not save himself. And God did not save Him. He died in such a terrible way. I close my eyes, remembering His agony, and it fills me with unspeakable grief!

I have never felt so alone. I have never felt such despair. I have never questioned my faith in the way that I do at this moment. I no longer know what to believe—or who to believe in.

I need to see Him one last time. There was no proper chance for grieving when it was all over and done. We prepared Him for burial with such haste, all before the sun went down. I need to touch His lifeless hand once more and look again at that loving face, even though His eyes are closed forever.

And I can be of service on this visit; I can bring myrrh and spices for anointing. We were so hurried that I went through the garden finding flowers to adorn Him, as we didn't have time to properly prepare His body for burial.

Somehow finding a task—a task that may still serve Him, even though He has departed—brings me comfort. It distracts me from my pain. It takes away, however briefly, all those sour thoughts of despair.

I will get up tomorrow, early in the morning, even as the dawn is breaking, and go back to His tomb.

REFLECTIONS AND PRAYERS

- ❖ Easter Saturday was undoubtedly Mary Magdalene's 'dark night of the soul'—a difficult time many of us undergo when our core beliefs and our faith are shaken. It makes us doubt ourselves and what we believe in.

- ❖ We all know that Mary Magdalene's despair is 'the darkness before the dawn'—the dawn of a joyful Easter Sunday when she becomes the first witness to the Resurrection. But throughout that Saturday, Mary had no idea what was about to happen the very next day. What does this teach us about navigating times of anguish, where all hope seems lost?

- ❖ Dear St. Mary Magdalene, pray for me when I find myself in despair, when I feel that I cannot cope. Show me that this is nothing more than the darkness before a beautiful dawn.

- ❖ Help me to find a task where I can do some good, a task that helps to ease my pain and sets me on a better path.

- ❖ Help me to find the hope I need, and share with me the joys of my Easter morning, when it comes, as I remember yours.

Easter Sunday

The Garden Tomb, East Jerusalem

A NOTHER SLEEPLESS NIGHT. It is yet dark, but I rise and prepare to go. Salome, Joanna, and Mary of Cleophas have all agreed to come with me. I am grateful for their company.

We walk through the darkness, along the stone road leading to the city gates. It is a solemn journey and we say little. I am careful with my oil lamp and the mixture of myrrh and spices that I carry in my jar. I have prepared them carefully, to perform one last service for the man who delivered me from terrible afflictions.

He was my teacher. He showed me a world that seemed to me the very Kingdom of God. But now, He is gone, and we are left to grieve. We are left with so many unanswered questions.

In the distance, the dawn is breaking. As we leave the city gates, I can see the terrible hill called Calvary where He was crucified. Just beyond it lies the garden where we laid Him. As we enter the garden, Mary asks, "Who will roll away the stone for us from the entrance of the tomb?" (Mark 16: 3–4)

She is right, of course. I hadn't thought of that! But when we arrive, the stone, which is very large and heavy, had already been rolled back. The tomb is open. I step down into it, holding my lamp carefully, trying to see in the darkness. But the tomb is empty! "They have taken Him away!" I call back to the others.

I start to weep yet again. Is it not enough to have put Him to death on a cross? Must they now take His body to an unmarked grave or a pit for brigands? "I will go to Peter" I tell them, and I hurry off, back to the city.

In the early morning light, I can see the lodgings where Peter has taken rooms, and I pound on the door. Someone I have never seen answers. No doubt they are being careful, as the high priests and Roman soldiers may be searching for them, too. "I'm Mary . . . of Magdala," I explain, out of breath. "I need to see Peter."

The man shakes his head. He's obviously been told to let on that he doesn't know Peter.

"I know he's here!" I raise my voice, "I've come from our Lord's tomb. He is gone!" An inner door opens and Peter, hearing my voice, comes out. He can see that I am trembling and upset. "They have taken the Lord out of the tomb, and we don't know where they have put Him." (John 20: 3–4)

Peter calls for John, the young disciple that Jesus loved, and I show them the way to the tomb. John can run much faster than Peter. He bounds ahead and gets there first.

I follow behind, unsure of what to do next. I had hoped this visit would bring me some measure of solace. Instead, it just brings more despair!

I can see John and Peter stepping down into the tomb. They will see, as I did, that there is nothing there. I walk back through the garden and find that the other women have all gone.

Before long, Peter and John come out again and now they seem excited. I can't understand why. They run back towards the city, passing me in their haste. But I remain outside the tomb, weeping and confused.

Finally, I stoop to look inside the empty tomb once again. There, I see two figures in white—like angels—sitting on the slab where His body had been, one at the head, the other at the feet. I am startled, but unafraid.

"Woman, why are you weeping?" one of them asks me.

"They have taken my Lord away," I reply. "And I don't know where they have put him." (John 20: 11–14).

Then I turn and see someone standing in the garden, just outside the entrance to the tomb. "Woman, why are you weeping?" he asks me. "Who are you looking for?" He must be the gardener. Perhaps he'll know what's happened.

"Sir," I reply, "if you have taken Him away, tell me where you have put Him and I will go and remove Him." (John 20: 15–16).

"Mary!" I hear my name, and I know the voice. How could this *be*? But without a doubt it *is*! It could be no one else. It is *Him*—standing there, outside the tomb, in the morning sun. "Rabboni—my teacher!" I gasp, reaching out to embrace Him.

He steps back and away from me, with a smile, "Do not cling to me," He tells me, "because I have not yet ascended to the Father. But go and find the brothers and tell them this: I am ascending to my Father and your Father, to my God and your God." (John 20: 17–18)

In that instant, a feeling of joy and peace the likes of which I have never known comes over me. He is alive! All that He said has come true! God *did* save Him in the end, and in a far more powerful way than I could ever have imagined. For He has overcome death—a horrible, treacherous death—and has come back to life! Here He is standing before me—speaking to me!

I don't want to leave His presence. I want to bask in it forever!

But He gestures towards the city gates. He wants me to go, to tell Peter, John and all the others this wonderful news.

Yet, Peter and John were here only moments ago. Why hadn't He appeared to them? Why did He wait and greet me, instead? Why did He choose me? I'll never know. Maybe it was because I'd stayed with Him—right to the end.

Then I run! I run back through the gates of the city and jubilantly down the cobblestone streets to Peter's lodgings. I pound on the door, filled with excitement.

When it opens, I see Peter, John, and many of the others, all looking at me anxiously. I take a moment to study their worried faces, to take it all in. Because I know that what I am about to say will fill them with joy and forever change their lives. What I am about to say will change the world.

"I have seen the Lord!"

WHAT DOES RECENT ARCHEOLOGY TELL US ABOUT MARY MAGDALENE?

The Discovery of Ancient Magdala

THE TOWN OF Magdala was destroyed during the Great Revolt in 67 CE, thirty-four years after the death of Jesus. Its ruins lay undisturbed thereafter for nearly two thousand years.

Ancient Magdala was finally rediscovered during a routine salvage dig by the Israeli Antiquities Authority (IAA) in 2009. The dig had been required in order to greenlight a construction project led by a Catholic priest who sought to build a pilgrimage center on the shores of the Sea of Galilee. He had chosen Magdala as the site for his project because of his mother's personal devotion to St. Mary Magdalene; this stemmed from a spiritual experience in her youth when she had been meditating upon Mary Magdalene's tremendous joy on the day of the Resurrection.

The priest, Father Juan Solana, had been acquiring land and raising money for the project since 2006. His blueprints were drawn and his construction crews hired. But under Israeli law, his team couldn't start work until the IAA had ascertained that nothing of historical significance would be impacted by the project.

A Prosperous and Devout Jewish Community

A few weeks into the Magdala dig, IAA archeologists struck a series of benches on the north side of Father Solana's property and unearthed a first century synagogue, buried only about a foot and a half beneath the surface. It had been undisturbed for nearly two millennia and nothing had ever been built on top of it.

It was the first synagogue ever found in the Galilee region dating from the time of Christ—even though the Gospel of Matthew tells us "Jesus went through Galilee, teaching in their synagogues, proclaiming the good news of the kingdom and healing every disease and sickness among the people" (Matthew 4:23). A coin from 29 CE discovered in its antechamber provides strong evidence that the synagogue was in operation during the time of Jesus' ministry.

The Magdala synagogue was luxuriously appointed. Beautiful mosaic tiles that had covered its floors were found intact along with fragments of a brightly-painted fresco. The most intriguing item found was a carved stone object about the size of a toy chest. It's known as the Magdala Stone. Many scholars believe that it served as a table for the reading of Torah scrolls. The stone appears to depict the interior of the Temple in Jerusalem. Whoever carved it—or ordered it to be carved—must have had access to the Temple's highly restricted inner sanctum.

The Beautiful First Century Synagogue Discovered at Magdala in 2009

Another unique find at the Magdala site are four Jewish ritual baths, known as *miqva'ot*. These utilize a sophisticated water system that was not seen again until the Middle Ages—yet another indication of the affluence of the Jewish community in first century Magdala. The presence of miqva'ots also suggests that the Jewish women of Magdala may have been quite modest, preferring to bathe privately rather than in the sea. It is not difficult to imagine Mary Magdalene immersing herself in one of these miqva'ots after Jesus released her from her demons and at other times in her life, when Jewish purification laws required it.

Jewish Ritual Bath or Miqva'ot
Where Mary Magdalene May Have Bathed

Where Did all the Money Come From?

Fish. Four ancient authors—Flavius Josephus, Cicero, Strabo and Suetonius—all mention the fame of Magdala's fish. The industry involved not only the sale of fresh fish, but dried, salted and pickled fish, along with fish paste and a popular fish sauce known as *garum*, may all have been exported from Magdala. Strabo, a first century Greek historian, wrote that the fish from Taricheae (Magdala's name in Greek) was highly esteemed in the markets of Rome.

Archeologists discovered a large, round fish pool over 40 feet in diameter close to the shoreline. This was likely used as a holding pool for catches offloaded from boats trawling the Sea of Galilee. There is also archeological evidence of glass manufacturing, including mobile ovens that would have supported this industry.

Magdala was not a backwater town with a few hardy fishermen out on the lake catching dinner for their families and food to sell to their neighbors. It was the center of a sophisticated agribusiness involving international trade.

Magdala's marketplace was sizeable for its time: twenty-eight shops were unearthed. Roughly three hundred fishing weights and over four thousand ancient coins have been found there, suggesting that a significant amount of foreign commerce took place, particularly through the port of Caesarea Maritime. From there, Magdala's fish would have been shipped to Rome and other markets throughout the Mediterranean. The fish from Magdala may have had the cachet of a gourmet product, somewhat akin to Norwegian smoked salmon today.

Magdala's economic prosperity from the fish industry created significant wealth for some of its citizens. Archeologists have discovered at least two large, multi-room dwellings referred to as mansions or villas not far from the marketplace. Their owners were undoubtedly of a high social strata.

Does This Mean that Mary Magdalene was Wealthy?

The archeological discoveries show that Mary Magdalene lived in a very prosperous town. But was she one of its elite? Or was she a poor prostitute who plied her trade with the town's many fishermen, as she has been characterized throughout history?

The best clue may lie not in the archeology but in the Bible, itself. As noted earlier, Luke (8: 1–3 and 24:10–11) tells us that Mary Magdalene was often in the company of Joanna, the wife of Herod's steward, Chuza.

It seems unlikely that a lady of Joanna's social rank would have been travelling about with a sex worker— even one who had repented her sins.

A more plausible scenario is that Mary Magdalene herself was a wealthy woman. It is notable that Mary is given prominence to Joanna when the women are listed in the gospel. While there may be many explanations for this, one is that Mary was a woman of even greater means and higher status than Joanna. She may have been the widow of a successful Magdala businessman or the heiress to a fortune based on the fishing industry.

Luke notes that the women who followed Jesus—Mary, Joanna, and the others—provided for him and the twelve "out of their own resources." If Mary was among the upper social classes of the town, the wealth of Magdala suggests that her resources may have been plentiful, indeed. The beautiful synagogue and sophisticated engineering of the Jewish ritual baths also give the impression that Magdala's affluent citizens commonly devoted resources to the furtherance of their religious beliefs and practices.

The Magdala synagogue itself raises some tantalizing prospects in this regard. It is very small in size—only 36 x 36 feet—and can accommodate only about two hundred people; the population of Magdala at the time was thought to be about four thousand, most of them Jewish.

Fragment from a brightly-painted fresco
that once adorned the Magdala Synagogue

Unlike most ancient synagogues, which are located near the town center, the Magdala synagogue was built on the town's northern edge, the part of the city closest to Capernaum. Was this lovely synagogue serving a small group of observant Jews who had become followers of Jesus?

In a 2016 interview with *Smithsonian Magazine,* Dr. Dina Avshalom-Gorni, the IAA archeologist who manages the Magdala dig, said it was her hunch that "no synagogue so small and finely decorated would have been built without some kind of charismatic leader."

Basin found in Ancient Magdala between the Marketplace and the Synagogue. Jesus might even have washed his hands here after coming to Magdala from Capernaum, a two-hour walk.

What About Those Seven Demons?

Some scholars are convinced that Mary Magdalene was the victim of true demonic possession, from which Jesus released her. Others believe that he cured her from epilepsy or another serious illness, possibly mental illness. The archeology at Magdala provides no insights into this long-standing question, however.

The only allusion to demons found at Magdala today is in the beautiful mosaic created by Chilean artist, Maria Jesus Ortiz de Fernandez, in the Mary Magdalene chapel. The mosaic pictured on the next page depicts the biblical references to Mary Magdalene as the woman from whom Jesus cast out seven demons (Luke 8:2, Mark 16:9).

The 2013 New York Times bestseller, *Brain on Fire: My Month of Madness* may offer an interesting possibility. Author Susannah Callahan describes her struggles with Anti-NMDA-receptor encephalitis, a neuropsychiatric syndrome associated with an ovarian teratoma or tumor. Callahan, a twenty-four-year-old journalist, began to experience numbness, seizures, hallucinations, movement disorders, and other psychotic symptoms.

Her boyfriend awoke to hear her emitting guttural-sounding grunts; she was having grand mal seizures, body spasms and slurring her words. Her limbs jutted out into unnatural positions. She lost consciousness and bit her tongue, causing blood to spurt from her mouth. She hallucinated about people aging right in front of her.

Doctors told Callahan that they believe this condition may have accounted for cases of demonic possession throughout history.

The illness affects about twenty thousand people every year in the United States today and is more common in women (80%) than men. While patients have ranged from twelve to over eighty years of age, it is most often found in women of child-bearing age.

MAGDALA TODAY: A PLACE THAT HONORS WOMEN

THERE IS PERHAPS no better place to honor women than Magdala—the ancient town on the Sea of Galilee where Mary Magdalene lived and with which she will always be associated.

Whether Mary Magdalene was rich or poor, beautiful or plain, youthful or elderly, devout and proper or someone with 'a past', what stands out is her character: her courage, her devotion, her determination, and her love. No doubt these same fine qualities—and others—characterized many women of the New Testament who followed Jesus and supported his work at a time when his teachings were considered unconventional—even radical.

Father Juan Solana, the Catholic priest whose efforts initiated the salvage dig that brought ancient Magdala to light, finally got to build his retreat center and guesthouse, the Magdala Center. Its design was re-worked to incorporate the archaeological excavations, which now attract thousands of tourists and pilgrims.

One of the loveliest features of the Magdala Center is a beautiful church called Duc in Altum, which means 'go out into the deep' a reference to the command Jesus gave Peter in Luke 5:4. It features an altar shaped like a boat, with the Sea of Galilee behind.

The Church at Duc in Altum, Magdala, Israel

Mary Magdalene's Stations of the Cross

But perhaps Duc in Altum's most delightful feature is its rotunda, known as the Women's Atrium. A golden mosaic banner that encircles the Atrium ceiling is inscribed with a Latin quote derived from the Letter on the Dignity of Women (#31) written by St. Pope John Paul II. It loosely translates as follows:

> *"In this holy place, the church gives thanks for the feminine genius, for the eternal dignity of women and for the great works God has done through them throughout history for humanity."*

The Women's Atrium is supported by eight marble columns, six of which are named for women mentioned in the New Testament:

- Mary Magdalene (Luke 8:2)
- Susanna and Joanna, the wife of Herod's steward, Chuza (Luke 8:3)
- Martha and Mary, the sisters of Lazarus, from Bethany (Luke 10:38)
- Salome, the mother of James and John, wife of Zebedee (Matthew 20:20)
- Mary of Cleophas (John 19:25)
- Simon-Peter's mother-in-law (Matthew 8:15)

A seventh column is dedicated to *Aliae Multae*—the many other women who supported Jesus. (Mark 15:41).

The eighth and final column is especially beautiful. It has been intentionally left blank. The Magdala Center explains: "One unmarked pillar stands for women of all time who love God and live by faith. Each woman can spiritually inscribe her own name as a poignant reminder of her role in the history of humanity."

The Women's Atrium, Duc in Altum, Magdala, Israel

A portion of the proceeds from sales of this book will be donated to the Magdala Project to continue the archeological excavation of ancient Magdala and the construction of the Magdala Center, which welcomes people from around the world to Mary Magdalene's hometown.

For more information on Magdala or to make your own personal donation in support of this work, please visit:www.magdala.org.

A Note from the Author: I really appreciate the time you took to read this book and sincerely hope that you enjoyed it. If you did, please consider leaving a review on your favorite book platform. If you'd like to reach me with any questions or comments, please email me at ann@annregimbal.com.

All best wishes to you!

BIBLIOGRAPHY

Station One

Maier, Paul. 1998. *Josephus: The Essential Writings*. Grand Rapids, MI: Kregel Academic and Professional.

Klein, Christopher. "Why Did Pontius Pilate Have Jesus Executed?" Accessed on www.history.com on April 16, 2019.

Station Six

Badde, Paul. 2016. *The Face of God: The Rediscovery of the True Face of Jesus*. San Francisco: Ignatius Press.

Gaspari, Antonio. "Has Veronica's Veil been Found?" Urbi et Orbi Communications. Accessed on CatholicCulture.org in February 2020. https://www.catholicculture.org/culture/library/view.cfm?recnum=2856

Station Thirteen

McAuley, Joseph. "A Letter to the Other Joseph in Jesus' Life: St. Joseph of Arimathea." *America: The Jesuit Review* (April 3, 2015). Accessed February 27, 2020. https://www.americamagazine.org/content/all-things/letter-other-joseph-jesus-life-saint-joseph-arimathea.

Gaskell, Simon. "Joseph of Arimathea Could be Buried in Cardiff, Claims Author". Wales Online. Accessed February 20, 2020. https://www.walesonline.co.uk/news/wales-news/christian-icon-joseph-arimathea-could-5164183

Station Fourteen

Pontifical Institute Notre Dame of Jerusalem Center. *Who is the man of the Shroud?* Permanent Exhibition. Accessed February 27, 2020. https://www.notre-damecenter.org/shroudexhibition

Avinoam, Danin. *Botany of the Shroud: The Story of Floral Images on the Shroud of Turin.* Jerusalem: Danin Publishing, 2010.

What Does Recent Archeology Tell Us About Mary Magdalene?

Callahan, Susannah. *Brain on Fire: My Month of Madness.* New York: Simon and Schuster, 2013.

García, Jesús. *The Magdala Project.* Gospa Arts, 2016.

Ristine, Jennifer. *Mary Magdalene: Insights from Ancient Magdala.* Published by author, 2018.

Sabar, Ariel. "Unearthing the World of Jesus," *Smithsonian Magazine.* January 2016. https://www.smithsonianmag.com/history/unearthing-world-jesus-180957515/. Accessed February 27, 2020.

Zapata-Meza, Marcela. "The Fishy Secret of Ancient Magdala's Economic Growth," *Bible History Daily*, August 9, 2016. Accessed February 27, 2020. https://www.biblicalarchaeology.org/daily/archaeology-today/the-fishy-secret-to-ancient-magdalas-economic-growth/

www.ingramcontent.com/pod-product-compliance
Lightning Source LLC
Chambersburg PA
CBHW042129100526
44587CB00026B/4234